Mosaics 3

Anthology of Short Stories and Poems of the
Women Writers Association of Central Illinois

Women Writers Association Executive Board
Kathleen O'Hara Podzimek
Linda McElroy
Celia Wesle

Mosaics Coordinator
Kathleen O'Hara Podzimek

Mosaics Editor
Anita Stienstra

Adonis Designs Press

Adonis Designs Press
P.O. Box 202
Chatham, Illinois 62629

Manufactured in the United States of America

ISBN: 978-0-9819750-5-4

Cover art by Kathleen O'Hara Podzimek
Book design by Anita Stienstra

Dedication

This is book is dedicated to the founding board of the Women Writers Association, and in particular to Kathleen O'Hara Podzimek. As a founding member of WWA in 1983, she has since taken the lead to keep members informed, recruit new members, and plan meetings, events, and publications. Thanks for all you do and for keeping the group alive, Kathleen.

CONTENTS

INTRODUCTION

Women Writers Association celebrates its 27th anniversary this year.

Over the years, we've encouraged members to write in their preferred styles, using their chosen perspectives and genres. This diversity of approaches has produced plays, essays, novels, poetry, short stories, movie scripts, interactive murder mysteries, and more.

During the years, we've also become good friends, helping each other through life changes including births, deaths, marriages, divorces, job changes, and retirements. The structure of monthly writers' meetings has remained the same throughout this time. A member hosts the meeting at her home and chooses a writing topic. The topic is then shared with members in advance of the meeting so that those who choose to do so can write to the topic before the meeting. At the beginning of the meeting, the hostess allots 25-30 minutes to write about the topic after which time members read what they wrote. The most fascinating outcome of this exercise is the diversity of approaches to the writings and the substantial amount of talent that is displayed during these readings.

After the group writing exercise, members share information concerning writing-related resources they've discovered. Topics have included titles of books which have proven valuable, upcoming training workshops and classes, grants that the group is eligible to apply for, publications to which they can pitch their writings, and more.

After this group information sharing, members read the writings they've been working on during the month. Before reading, the writer tells group members what she's looking for in terms of feedback. The request could be for general comments or advice regarding particular aspects of the writing, such as voice or style, opening/closing paragraphs, selection of titles or writing markets.

During the meeting, members are tactful about sharing advice. We stress positive feedback and suggest changes when writers request it so that the support group environment is comfortable and relaxed.

In closing, we hope you enjoy reading this anthology. Our writings have been grouped around topics explored by members during the past four years. Topics in this issue include: I Died in Paris on a Rainy Afternoon, Treasuring Our Memories, Summer Memories, A Character from Your Past, As the Past Fades, Legends of the Fall, Mysteries/Family Secrets, Always Wonder, Springtime, True Sisters, and Reality/Illusions.

Now it is your turn to enjoy the diversity of styles and the talents that our members demonstrate and perhaps spark some creativity of your own. Thank you for supporting the arts by purchasing this anthology.

Linda McElroy, Kathleen O'Hara Podzimek, Celia Wesle
Governing Board Members
Women Writers Association

I Died in Paris on a Rainy Afternoon in Early Spring

Angel
painting
Kimberly Magowan

I Died in Paris

I died in Paris on a rainy afternoon in early spring. It was a Thursday and tickets for an excursion on the Seine were half price. Being a smart shopper, I was eager to take advantage of this bargain for Paris was much more expensive than I had anticipated. Unfortunately, I had not understood how converting dollars to euros would deplete my funds so quickly.

As I boarded the boat, I noticed that the other passengers seemed remarkably large. "Bon jour, madame," said the steward, "we have two tour groups on board today. From Japan, we have members of the Sumo Wrestler Academy and from Germany the Society of Gourmands of Munich."

Feeling especially svelte in my new Parisian raincoat and hat, I took a deck chair and prepared to enjoy a relaxing, all be it damp, afternoon. All was well until the tour guide began to speak in Japanese, at which half my fellow passengers rushed to one side of the boat. When he repeated the message in German, the others crowded to the same side. As the deck began to tilt, my chair slid to join them. Pandemonium ensued as instructions were shouted in Japanese, German, and French, and I struggled to recall enough high school French to understand.

As I hit the water and began to sink, l remembered one French phrase that seemed particularly apt: Je suis morte. *

Linda McElroy

*Translation: I am dead.

No Accounting for Taste

I, Renee Gairden, died in Paris on a rainy afternoon in early spring. It was a Thursday. I tried touching my body but couldn't. I wondered if I had eyes. I could see but couldn't blink.

Straining, I saw a white light. The light was astonishingly beautiful, an oddly white kind of sunset, with touches of silvers, eggshells, and brilliant golds. I rushed towards the light, actually flying, just like I'd always dreamed of, but wait…what about my husband? He must be in mortal danger. I have to help him.

I looked down, searching for Jean-Paul. He was in an alley bent over me. My eyes were open, staring at nothing. Jean-Paul gently closed my eyes, hugging me, rocking me in his arms, crying.

We'd celebrated my birthday at Jacques Restaurant one block off of Champs-Elysees near the Seine. It was an upscale restaurant with an expansive court yard. We'd dined on duck a la orange while listening to Beethoven and enjoying the night air.

Afterwards, Jean-Paul said that he'd meet me at our apartment. He wanted to shop at the wine story for Korbel champagne and gorgonzola cheese. He told me to go ahead and let our dog Zoë out.

I headed home, feeling a bit giddy, thinking about the evening ahead, sitting on our tiny balcony, enjoying the night air, sipping champagne, in the company of the man I loved. The night was illuminated by a full moon, bouncing its brilliant rays off the Seine. Gorgeous.

I walked on the cobblestone sidewalk past stores and bricked apartment buildings on my right, the river on my left. Crossing an alley, my high heel stuck in a crevice between the cobblestones. Out of the corner of my eye, I noticed a tall man with long hair. Turning around, I saw that the man had moved next to me. I looked into eyes the color of coal. He bent down, removing my heel from the crevice then picked me up and carried me, screaming, into the alley.

I wanted to freeze but willed myself to fight, thinking that Jean Paul couldn't be far behind. He was strong. He'd be here soon.

The attacker found a sheltered place between large garbage cans to lay me down. I smelled something putrid nearby like rotting vegetables. He lay on top of me, his long black hair caressing my neck. I tried pushing him off but he was too strong.

All I could think of was that he was going to rape and then kill me. I had to do something. I wiggled, trying to free a hand so that I could grab something to hit him with. It didn't work. I couldn't budge.

He closed his eyes and began kissing me on my forehead, then my cheeks, then on my lips. His touch was so gentle that I felt myself responding. No, I thought, don't go there.

He slid down, lightly kissing my neck. It felt so good that I felt guilty…where was my husband? Jean-Paul should have been here by now. Why wasn't he here, getting this man off me?

The man continued kissing then licking my neck. I groaned without wanting to. He then opened his mouth widely and bit me. That was the last thing I remembered.

I have to get back to Jean-Paul. This man will kill him next.

Jean-Paul was now laying my body down while looking closely at my neck. He saw the tooth marks. His face was puzzled. He was still crying.

I have to get back to Jean-Paul. He's in mortal danger.

I tried willing myself out of the light. As I concentrated on leaving, I felt pain in my neck or was I imagining it? I felt my hand moving toward my neck. My eyes opened slightly to look at my husband.

Jean-Paul's tears of grief turned to tears of joy. He held me, kissing me, rocking me, saying, "Renee, you've come back, thank God!"

It was at that point that I bit him.

Kathleen O'Hara Podzimek

12

I HAVE DIED AGAIN TODAY

forgive me Lord
for i have died again today

followed you too close
tiptoed into your wake
so i could stand
in the crevice of time

forgive me Lord
your absence hurts

i feel too much
i know you too well
i'm pulled out toward the edge
like ink diffusing into cloth

my feathers spread too soon

forgive me Lord
i will rise Lazarus-like
tuck in my corners
and emit my being back to life

Anita Stienstra

MESMERIZED

I mesmerize about Paris in the spring, with a cute flirty umbrella dashing around puddles with long wavy flowing hair, the sun glistening off a block of my locks at just the right angle, the right time. Of course, my long, tall lover is next to me in this exercise. He too has black hair that glistens. His smile is loaded with the lust of the eye, the pride of life.

My journeys across the oceans have taken me to Paris in the year 2000 by accident as we were bound for Africa, the land of the Asante' people. We missed a connection, detouring on a later flight to the Charles de Gaulle airport. As the missed connection was the airline's fault, we were wined and dined, compliments of British Airways with a layover of several hours. Although preference would have been to have a true Parisian experience, seeing the red plush carpet, soft lighting and having several drinks in the British Airways Club was the extent. I wish now we had included in our trip to Africa a two-three day overstay in Paris. That would have sufficed my dreams.

Jennifer C. Herring

Treasuring Our Memories

Poochie on the Rocker
pen on paper
Celia Wesle

TREASURING OUR MEMORIES

Summer swimming
at Esterbrook Park
in the Milwaukee River,
usually a long sunny day
that raised a big blister
across my shoulders and back.

The boys pointed at me
"Watch out; she's a tough one!"
was said. I was honored.
I was effectively
protecting my little sister
from their pushing and dunking.

I loved the sand and
I learned to stretch out on the towel
in my blue wool swim suit.
I dared to jump feet first
from a very high diving board.
Became a camp waterfront director.

Celia Wesle

TREASURING OUR MEMORIES

Riding back from Grandma's,

Four kids in the backseat of a '50 Chevy

Mom and Dad murmuring in front while

Baby brother's sweaty head bobs on my shoulder,

I watch a shadow auto chasing the harvest moon

And sing "Cry Me a River" in my sultry soprano.

Linda McElroy

Photo by Ruth Heckathorn in Costa Rico

IN FLIGHT

We sat in the backyard, a sunny day, watching the hummingbirds flittering around Linda's feeders. The hummingbirds looked like iridescent jewels sparkling in the air. Their translucent wings moved swiftly as they hovered in space. They flew between feeders strategically placed among beds of red hibiscus and trumpet creepers.

Ruth sat, peering through binoculars, transfixed. She smiled, watching them flying backwards and sideways, radiating like hot coals in the sun. She leaned against the lawn chair, her back as straight as a dancer's.

"In springtime, the hummingbirds come," she said.

And so the hummingbirds came every year to Linda's garden, and every year we sat in her backyard watching them, their iridescent colors dazzling us.

One year, Ruth asked, "Did you know hummingbirds migrate two thousand miles to visit us?" The following year, she went bird watching to Costa Rico. When she returned, we viewed photos of brilliantly-hued birds.

"Did you know that hummingbirds are little more than flight muscles covered with feathers?" she asked.

"Oh," Linda said, "they're like you...muscled, but feathery." Linda liked to tease.

Over the years, Linda and I learned about hummingbirds. Linda asked, "Did you know that a hummingbird's flight speed averages 25-30 mph?" Ruth, who competed in marathons, said, "If I keep practicing, perhaps I can out run them."

And so the years went on until one day, the three of us were sitting in Linda's garden when Ruth said, "I found a lump on my breast; I'm going to the doctor."

Later, Ruth said, "They found breast cancer. Did you know that most hummingbirds die in the first year of life?"

On weekends, Linda drove Ruth to monthly doctor's appointments in Evanston. I went with Ruth to doctors in Springfield during the work week as my hours, working from home, were flexible. Taking her to doctor's appointments became an activity we enjoyed doing because we loved Ruth so much.

During appointments, Ruth asked me to take notes. The oncologist, Ruth, and I developed a playful banter during appointments. I'd ask the doctor how to spell a medical term or prescription drug; she'd laugh, and then tell me. I'd write it down after which Ruth would say, "Are you sure you're getting that down correctly, Kathleen?"

After one appointment, Ruth asked, "Did you know hummingbirds can flash their bright colors as well as hide them when needed?"

"No, I didn't know that," I said. "Is that what you're doing with the doctors...hiding your sharp mind from their view?"

Over a two-year period, the cancer spread to Ruth's pelvis and liver. We went to chemotherapy and radiation treatment sessions. During those times, Ruth asked the oncologist questions as though she was reviewing the results of one of her research projects. I tried to respond in the same way.

A year into treatment, Ruth built up enough courage to ask the doctor, "How long will I live?"

"I'd say six months or less," the oncologist said.

After we left the doctor's office, we hugged each other and cried. Ruth said, "The oldest known hummingbird was a broad-tailed hummingbird, tagged 12 years apart. I won't live that long."

As the disease progressed, Esther, Ruth's sister, moved into her house to take care of her. One day, Esther asked Linda and me to come over, saying that she needed our help.

Esther had been trying to get Ruth to take morphine to ease her breathing problems but Ruth refused because she'd read that taking the drug could shorten the number of days she had left.

When we arrived, we were surprised to find Ruth's oncologist sitting beside Esther at the kitchen table. Esther was sitting across from Ruth, in a wheelchair, looking sallow, on oxygen, gasping for air. A faint smile crossed Ruth's face when she saw Linda and me.

The oncologist told Ruth that she was dying and that she had a choice. She could continue refusing to take morphine to ease her breathing problem or die a painful death, gasping for air.

Ruth looked at her sister and said, "What do you think, Esther?" but Esther didn't respond.

"Heh, girl," I said, moving to Ruth's side, taking her hand. Ruth twitched her finger in response.

Choking back tears, I said, "A hummingbird will take about 250 breaths per minute while at rest. Why don't you take some medicine to slow your breathing down so you can rest, too?"

Later that day, Ruth took the morphine. The morphine slowed-down her breathing so she could rest. And, on the following morning, she died. It was a cold day in February when she left us.

*****

The following April, a young woman stood in the foyer of Denney's Restaurant at the time we had agreed to. Wearing an Elizabethan hat and velvet dress, she smiled at Linda and me as she pulled out a piece of paper from her beaded purse.

"I have a message," she said. "A close friendship is like a priceless diamond—valuable, precious, and hard to break."

Who was this strange woman and why was she doing this? I wondered. I glanced at Linda. She shrugged. Apparently Linda didn't know either.

Going into her purse again, the woman pulled out two hand-painted boxes. "Gifts from a friend," she said, and left.

Linda and I went inside the restaurant, ordered coffees, and opened the gift boxes. Typed notes inside the boxes read, "In springtime, hummingbirds come." Under the notes were ceramic hummingbird pins with diamond eyes.

We now knew who had sent this strange woman and the gifts. We laughed and cried and held each other's hands. Linda repeated the message, "In springtime, hummingbirds come."

I responded, "Did you know hummingbirds will migrate two thousand miles to visit us?

Finally, we smiled. It was springtime. The hummingbirds would return every year like fond memories that hover and soar but whose beauty is forever with us, just like Ruth.

Kathleen O'Hara Podizmek

VISIONS

grasping the spread

she clutched the

wrinkled past

as if to wrest it

from a devil of

diminished memory

unfinished memory—

down she lay

her silver head

to pray

bright and

infinite visions

Jean Staff

Summer Memories

Gull Watching Light
photograph
Anita Stienstra

Summer Memories

The candles flicker as the breeze gently presses lightly on my skin, blowing the lavender scent my way.

The string of lights lining the ceiling of our screened-in room feature red and green peppers and sombreros.

Looking out, night cloaks the oak tree in black, leaving the outline of its branches splayed about, and cutting through the darkness at angles worthy of an artist's brush.

I lay in the settee, snuggling in my favorite throw, feet tucked in, head resting on throw pillows, savoring the sights and smells.

Our dog, KeeKee, yawns, grunts, and flops down on the floor. My husband, Ray says, "Isn't it delightful being back in the screened-in room again?"

Kathleen O'Hara Podzimek

THE PEBBLED PATH

One day a little boy was playing on the beach.
He decided to make a sandcastle.
So he gathered pebbles and created a path in a very special place;
a place that no one could get to.

And then he built his sandcastle.
It was very simple, but beautiful.

And then the waves came—
and washed it away.

The boy grew up.
He became a teenager.
One day he was walking on the beach and found the path of pebbles
he had built as a child.
He decided to build another sandcastle on the pebbled path.

He took with him what he remembered when he built the sandcastle as
a child. He remembered the wet sand and how it pressed together to
help him create his castle.
But this time he added something more.
He added windows
so that he could see the waves rushing in toward his castle.
It was beautiful.

Then the waves came—
and washed it away.

Years later the teenager became a man.
One day he was walking on the beach and to his surprise he noticed that
the path of pebbles was still there after all of these years.
He smiled in amazement.
He decided to build a new sandcastle.
This time, however, it was different.
He added something more…something that could never be destroyed,
broken, or washed away…
…only disappear for a short time.
He began to remember

when he was a child the wet sand and how it pressed nicely together.
He remembered as a teenager how he added a lot of detail and windows
so that he could see the beauty in front of him,
even though he knew it would soon wash away.

But this time he also added a door—an opened door,
so that when the waves came rushing in, unexpectedly,
he could walk through the door and be safe.

But he would also take with him something else.
He would take all of the beautiful moments—the moments he made
beautiful as a child and as a teenager;
the moments worth remembering, even though they didn't last long.
For in each of those moments there was joy that never washed away.

The sun gently touched his face in the dim room through the curtains.
The man was old now.

He had a difficult time remembering. The man had not spoken in years.

A loving hand touched his hand.

It just happened to be their 50th anniversary.
They weren't celebrating, however, with an extravagant party,
or a lot of gifts.

They celebrated with much more;

one heart speaking to the next
…without words.

And then it happened—
…another moment.

He spoke.

"What did you say?" she asked. "Did I hear you say…'I love you'?"

The man didn't reply.
He smiled.

At that moment he opened his hands, and cupped gently in his palms,
was a castle made of sand.
It was carved with detailed windows
and an opened door.

A tear streamed down her face.
She could hear him clearly, even though he wasn't speaking.
As she looked at the castle she understood what he was telling her.

The pebbled path led him to her.
All of the castles he built were washed away.
But the most beautiful castle is the one they share now—
in this moment.
It is the castle the pebbled path led them to.
The castle that held all of the moments—
The joy felt within each one.
The joy of feeling the wet sand and how it pressed together to help him
create his castle,
even though he knew it would soon wash away.

It was the joy of creating a lot of detail and windows
so that he could see the beauty in front of him,
even though he knew it would soon wash away.

This was the castle the pebbled path led them to.
It was the castle that held all of the moments.
The most beautiful castle that couldn't be seen,
and could never wash away.

It was on the path all along.
He just couldn't see it at the time.

The castle was secure.
It had windows to see beautiful moments—the little things—
ordinary miracles,
like the one they share now.

The castle with an opened door
that kept him safe
and allowed love to find him
on the pebbled path that never ends.

Kimberly K. Magowan

27

SUMMER MIDDAY ON THE POND

Lulled by lap, silk upon her bank,
still lies morning pond
—senses vagabond.
By noon her sandy ass winces rosy,
winces randy and sore
with sun's spank.
Swaddled Bobolink, so nest cozy,
chirp chirps a snore.
In waddled grass,
duck royal does nap
with nary a thought that dog, cat
and brat...do not.

Maiden flowers, manifold,
winking, they tease
the   frantic showers
of bold bachelor bees
aswirl, atwirl
the red, gold, the please,
and stink, of the girl musky curl.
To nimbus cloud,
pink nippled thru white chiffon,
moppet willows bawl for a drink,
as old granny breeze, cognac tippled,
stifles a salty yawn.

Then see them crawl,
their green skin rippled,
the jump high crowd
with mump-eye faces that stare
and plump-thigh legs that sprawl
lily pad pillows.
Beware! By blink unseen,
shadows slink serpentine
thru the foxtail tall and blonde,

thru the rosette veil of steam.
While far beyond
the pale of pole and net,
fishes sink into unfathomed wet
Dream—Summer Midday on the Pond.

Jean Staff

AT PERDIDO BEACH

Our first morning at the beach. A cup
of black coffee steams beside me. You
tilt your head, blow Marlboro Light rings,
then take a swig of Gatorade. I point
out a boat maneuvering through the bay,
its westward-bent sail opalescent as last
night's crescent moon. Dominating
everything is the incessant shriek of
seagulls and the pounding of the surf.

While you take your shower, I lean
against the railing and watch a young
couple, holding hands, wade barefoot
through rolling breakers. I shudder
when I see a cluster of teenagers,
sporting cool sunglasses, kick
a multi-colored ball around and around,
barely missing the self-absorbed couple.
Then I see a woman herd three excited
youngsters laden with buckets
and shovels across the courtyard, past
palm trees shaped like Havana cigars
and purple martin houses swarming
with early birds. I watch them cross
the sand and settle near the water,
presumably to spend the morning
digging moats and building castles.
Without warning, just as you emerge

from the bathroom, an orange excavator
right below our balcony revs its engine
and, clanking like a rusty tank, transports
an awkward scoop-held, moon-buggy-like
contraption toward the furthest edge
of the beach. Why? Don't they know
it's Saturday? And we're on our first
and only vacation of the year?

Pat Martin

THE ILLINOIS SUN

The Illinois sun
gleams deep
pumpkin-orange
beams tangerine-red
seems to swirl
peach and mango
and I feast my eyes
and feel hungry—
hungry with delight.

This is the Illinois sun
when it sets
when it sits
on a strip
of white horizon
a huge ball balanced
on flat earth
before it fades.

It appears you too
may disappear
in the front seat
of this car
as you stoop
and jiggle back and forth
to catch
one last glimpse
in the side view mirror.

Anita Stienstra

FOR THE KINDNESS OF STRANGERS

It was a Thursday before Mother's Day and my life was just right. The flowers were blooming, birds were singing, and people were acting like they had spring fever. A committee of my peers had just voted yes to my promotion to the rank of full professor at the university in Illinois. Professor with a big "P" is as high as one can go in academe unless you want to become a dean, provost, chancellor, or president. Neither job interested me.

In the promotion application, I pontificated about the *nobility* of teaching students to help others; of preparing them to give of themselves for the good of humankind; and of the value of giving with no expectation for appreciation from the people we serve. I was pretty proud of myself. My chest was all puffed up.

I scheduled the Friday off from my clinical practice and headed to Mississippi to visit my family. The two days were restorative and completely uneventful, but the return trip taught me how much work I still have to do to understand people.

At a rest stop 100 miles into trip, I checked the gas gage mentally noting that I would need gas very soon. I reached for my purse and discovered it missing. Panic and fear yanked at my senses as I did a mental scan and realized I had left the purse on the front porch of my mother's house. I was too far from my home in Illinois to make it without running out of gas and too far away from my mother's house to return without running out of gas. I searched the glove compartment and my pockets but found only loose change. With no cash and no plastic, what was I to do? Panic set in as I realized what a predicament I was in. Here I was, a big time doctor from Illinois, riding in a fancy foreign car, wearing diamond earrings and an expensive watch, out in the middle of Arkansas and with no idea how to get a couple of gallons of gas.

Panic rose from my stomach, moved up into to my chest and throat, and cut my breath to a fast shallow pant. I started the car thinking the distraction of driving would clear my head. I tried to form a plan while watching the gas gage drop seemingly more quickly than before. Distracting thoughts took me to one of our class discussions where a student talked about how the American society shows disdain and disrespect for poor people. If they are in need, they must be lazy and trying to con someone out of something. Malingering is the word, I told her. Another student reminded her of economic advantages of poverty and misery. "We make our living on other people's misery," she said. "As long as there are poor, lonely, depressed, unhappy and angry people, we have job security."

I pulled into a Shell gas station in Osceola, Arkansas thinking I'd call the state police and seek their advise. When I told the clerk about my predicament, the station manager suggested, with a bit of contempt in her voice, that I should try the mission down the street—a ready answer I thought, for anyone black. Surely she must know I'm not mission material. I could feel a panicky feeling again but this time it was in response to her HAUGHTY, overbearing self pride. I wanted to put my fist through her face with that pink mouth and missing teeth. But I didn't. Too often I face and easily still tire of people and their prejudiced reactions to me and people who look like me. Prejudice and discrimination create a kind of tension that makes me want to pee.

While in the bathroom, I decided the state police was probably my best bet. But, when I returned to the bathroom a woman on the station's staff handed me $21. They had collected it from each other, including $3 from Pink Lips. Relieved and happy, I could buy enough gas to drive back to my mother's house, get my purse and return to their station for a fill-up.

I returned to the station a few hours later, gave them their $21 and added a bonus for my own conscience. They were gracious about the bonus but not surprised at my return.

I thought about those women on both legs of the trip. Why did they do it? Working at a gas station on a Mother's Day, they surely had little money, and families who needed every penny they could make. I could have been a con, preying on other people. How could they know I am an honest person? Maybe they could see the real distress I was experiencing and knew I was for real. Or, is what I've heard true, that the poorest people are the most generous? I guess I'll never know for sure.

Of all the women there that day, I was probably changed the most. I was impressed by their generosity and humility and vowed to be kinder and more patient with other people.

I travel that highway often going to visit my family. I decided to get a cell phone just in case I had another such emergency. But now, each time I pass the Shell station in Osceola, Arkansas, I experience *very* warm feelings.

Rachell N. Anderson

GENEROSITY

Wide driveway still-life
Of elegant objects
Until 8 a.m. crowd.
Cathy's giving heart
Eased garage sale toil.
Rather than valuing
Deciding and applying
Hundred of tags
Offer: Everything one dollar
All plates and goblets
Chair, chests
All: plain or beautiful
Will be rewarded many-fold.
House is emptied
Of all not needed.
Inveterate bargainer
Offers fifty cents
For beautiful blanket.
"Sure," says the householder.
Designer of customer miracles.

Celia Wesle

A Character
From Your Past

Photo provided by Kathleen O'Hara Podizmek

MARY MARGARET'S STORY

Looking at me, your first impression would be of austerity: fine, thin gray hair pulled back into a knot, no makeup, wearing a housedress, worn but clean. I could be described as a "slip of a woman," standing five feet five inches tall, weighing 100 pounds. Now, in the year of our Lord 1950, being over 65 years old, I'm still straight as a board. Few remember me when I was a young vibrant woman with thick, lustrous dark hair and rosy cheeks. I keep emotions to myself. You'll see no reaction from me from what you say other than a silent acknowledgment of your presence, staring straight at you from clear blue eyes. My emotions are my private stock, and I will not let myself be hurt again.

As a young woman, I opened my heart and trusted that my feelings would be respected, but that was a mistake I vowed never to make again. As long as I can control my emotions, I am in control of my life. If ever the tears begin to fall, the strong walls I have built could be washed away in a flood of sorrow.

My name is Mary Roche. I'm first generation Irish, having arrived in America from County Limerick at age 15. I now live at 123 South Richmond Street in Chicago with my brother, children, and grandchildren. My home is a two-story bungalow with a full basement on a corner lot. I bought the home so that we'd have a nice place to live. We do all right. I am the mother hen with her flock close at hand. Having the family together is all that matters in the end.

My daughter May lives on the first floor with me. May is a rounder version of me with the same clear blue eyes and regular features. She's the first woman manager of Union Pacific Railroad. I'm proud of her and frequently tell her so. However, I don't brag about her to strangers. May is the fashion plate in our family and loves decorating our home. "Everything needs to be just so," so says May. My son, Maurice, also lives with us. He works at City Hall. He sometimes comes straight home from work, sometimes not. He enjoys playing cards with his friends. He's handsome which makes the ladies go after him. However, Maurice isn't interested. He loves his mother too much, I guess. Some might say that he's a Momma's boy, but if he is, there are worse things that could happen to him. I will never break his heart.

On the second floor, my youngest, Margaret lives with her husband, Francis Gerald O'Hara (he prefers Jerry O'Hara), and their four children. Margaret has my slim body but is more athletic and taller. In fact, at five foot 10 inches, she's taller than most men. I tell Margaret to stand up straight and be proud of her height. Sometimes she listens.

Her husband, Jerry, is over six feet tall. He's a lawyer and real estate broker who works for himself. He sees himself as good looking but he really isn't. That's all right though; better to have too much confidence than too little. As men go, he's okay.

While not practicing law or selling houses, Jerry volunteers for the Holy Name Society and bowls with Our Lady of Sorrows League. He also spends a great deal of time sitting in his easy chair, reading the *Chicago Tribune* and listening to sports on the radio. It bothers me that he doesn't help Margaret with the housework or the children but that is how men are. He's a good man otherwise; he keeps food on the table for his family.

Margaret and Jerry have four children, three girls— Maureen, Kathleen, and Eileen—and one boy, Brian James. They're good children and I love them all, but they are a handful, as you can imagine.

I help Margaret whenever I can. When Margaret goes bowling with her lady friends, I baby sit. When she goes to meetings of the Holy Rosary Society, I baby sit. I also sometimes cook more than May, Maurice, and I need, and take the food upstairs to Margaret's family. She doesn't like to cook and I don't mind helping out. Our lives are intertwined and we help each other like families are meant to.

My brother John converted a corner of our unfinished basement into a bedroom for himself. He makes his living as a fireman and spends his time away from work reading history books or making wooden toys and furniture.

He enjoys being with my grandchildren. John gives them pennies if they eat bone marrow because he says that bone marrow helps keep their bones strong. I don't know if this is true or not. It can't hurt them though and it makes John happy.

I'll backtrack now because my granddaughter Kathleen, who has endless questions, just came upstairs with something on her mind regarding my younger days. As she walked in the back door, I was working my Singer through the fabric of a recital dress for her sister, Maureen. There is always work to do. My hands are never idle. Here's the story.

When I was 25 years old, my five brothers—all public servants, policemen and fireman and city hall workers—put their cash together so that I could start a grocery store with me as the sole owner. I named the store County Limerick Store because I thought the name would please my brothers and it did. They made sure that I would be able to support my family. Family helping family. They knew I would work hard to make the store a success and I did. For years, I'd walk a block from our home on Richmond Street to the store at the corner of Jackson and Richmond to go to work.

I'd start at 4:00 a.m. making bread, fudge, cakes, cookies, and other confectionaries. The working men would stop by the store from 5:00 a.m. on, purchasing coffee and slices of hot fresh bread with my special orange marmalade and mounds of butter piled on top. The men would sit around the pot-bellied stove, trading news and gossip, then head to work. I enjoyed listening to them, hearing snippets of the neighborhood and city news.

Several men wanted to court me, but I wasn't interested in another man. One was Joe Burnaski, a butcher at Harnesty; another was Pat Gelesby who drove the bus on the rails in the early morning. Another was Jim Flaherty, a rather handsome man, a widow who had trouble keeping jobs. The more I ignored them, the more interested they became in me. It's ironic because although there was no husband in my house, his presence never left my heart.

As I mentioned earlier, Kathleen interrupted my musings while I was sewing. Just like a child to do that, isn't it?

"Grandpa really didn't' die, did he?" she asked. Kathleen was whispering as if someone was in the room, eavesdropping.

"Kathleen, how did such a thought get into your head?" I asked. Her intensity told me that she would not give up the question.

"It came from talking with Eileen," she said. "We think you don't want another man because the first one was bad."

"T'aint true," I lied. God forgive me. You see, some family history is better left unsaid.

The truth is that, when the gentlemen asked me out, I told them that my husband, Patrick died when my daughter Margaret was only two years old. I told them that I was a widow but that was a lie.

My husband did not live up to my hopes and dreams. He, in fact, was a nor-do-well—a woman chaser who liked the drink. I told him to go away. It was something that would send me to hell according to the Pope and the priests and the sister at Our Lady of Sorrows Church. God forgive me but I did it anyway.

I never saw him again. I hoped that he would miss me and the children enough to change his ways and come home, but he never did. I was right to throw him out before he hurt me or the children. Although I did not know if he was alive or dead during those years, I kept the love for the young man I married in my heart and never broke my wedding vows.

*****

Ten years later, when my time was short, I called Kathleen in to see me. I asked her what she thought of her odd, old grandmother. Kathleen took my hand and told me that she still doesn't believe my story about grandpa dying but that she loves me anyway.

"That's how it should be," says I, and then I left this world.

Kathleen O'Hara Podizmek

Note: This story is supposition. Mary Margaret and her brothers consistently said that grandmother was a widow.

WHO AM I

She saw herself as an ugly child with dishwater hair and a una-brow who dressed in little girl frocks and horn-rimmed glasses; a thin gangly, flat chested and flat butted, pale and pimpled freak biting her nails and praying herself away. She still had smooth underarms and legs and only wisps of pubic hair. Boys called her toothpick, ugly butt, and string bean, baby, smart ass.

Oh to have olive smooth skin, almond eyes, and a bubble butt like Margie, whom boys called a flirt; tight clothes, a signature walk, and 34 D's like Diane, whom the boys called sexy; platinum hair, long dark lashes and long nails like Carol, whom the boys called beautiful.

Her 14th summer, her body had not developed. She ate until she was sick and rejoiced in a two pound weight gain. She ordered a padded bra and padded girdle from Fredericks of Hollywood. Adapting to the clothes like her friends she wore pencil skirts, tight sweaters, bobby socks and saddle oxfords. She baked in the sun to darken her skin and shaved her underarms, legs, and pubis, to stimulate hair growth, succeeding only in always having toilet paper shreds hanging from various cuts. She disguised them with band aids. She conditioned and bleached her hair beige blond. It became her crowning glory. After much experimentation, she learned about skincare, to pluck her eyebrows and apply make up: foundation gave her a palette, blush and eye shadow a brightness, eyeliner gave her almond eyes, mascara a pop and with false eyelashes she practiced flirting. Trading in her horn-rims for contact lenses, the large old-fashion kind, she spent two months with watery eyes adapting to them. She stopped biting her nails, tending and cultivating them like Mother did her garden of roses. She replaced one bad habit with another—smoking non filtered Lucky Strikes, thinking it went with her new look.

This was not a smooth transition as it involved a lot of trial and error. During this time, boys and some girls called her new names: slut, whore, clown. She endured this ridicule and more, because she could see improvement.

By the age of 16, her looks consumed her life. Her grades dropped from A's to D's. She refused to shower in gym or change clothes in front of anyone fearing some one would notice her shortcomings. She wore her padded bra even beneath her pajamas. She tried to be perfectly coiffed and made up at all times. Her fingers were turning yellow and she smelled bad. However, other girls said she was cool; family told her she was pretty as a picture; boys and grown men whispered, "Hi, beautiful." And she had a boy-friend.

Yet she lived in constant fear of being found out, her inner voice shouting, "Fake, Fraud!" Worst of all, she did not feel real. She did not know how to go forward or backward. Skimming through a Cosmo, she found one of the many tests popular in that era. It looked simple enough. Answer the question, "Who am I?" three ways. Example: I am a woman, a person, a student.

She asked herself, "Who am I?"

I found no answer to that until I was in my forties.

Jean Staff

MY LOVE'S NOT A RED OR WHITE ROSE

They tied your shadow

to a pole

let loose the light.

Narcissus floats in the pond.

My narcissus floats in the pond.

My lover floats in a pond

like a fake cloud on water

untouchable by anything but

the past's pain and the future's promise.

Anita Stienstra

HUS-BAND

The home-ball rolls
Toward its sun,
I roll up the kitchen window shade and
Welcome it;
As I look, my cells awaken further
From gut to hand and foot;
A minute ago
In our house and bed,
I rolled toward my husband
With desire to bond;
He now comes into the room
Smiles gently, remembering, saying
"Want to play ball?"
The earth, our world, rolls on.

Celia Wesle

As the Past Fades

Garden Stuff Under Fractured Glass
pastel on canvas with glass
Celia Wesle

THE WAY OF THE SNAIL

The wheels on the bus go round and round
life does that to you
back to ground zero, back to square one.
Hope keeps alive, and does not disappoint.
It has not happened yet, but keep hoping, it will.
Tribulations make the wheels keep turning
round and round they go.
Striving for the best way, the better life.

Jennifer C. Herring

As usual, the trouble started when I got in too much of a hurry.

My husband Pete and I had just bought our dream house. To ensure maximum efficiency on moving day, I had planned to take our cats to the vet and board them for a few hours so they wouldn't be underfoot. I discovered the hard way that getting kitties into a carrier is not a process one can speed up without trauma to both cat and human. Olaf went into his carrier peacefully, but Champagne balked.

Keeping an eye on the clock, I grabbed Champagne and tried—ever so gently—to force him into the carrier. The same sweet kitty who had snuggled into my lap just moments earlier transformed himself into a growling, hissing ball of teeth and claws. I was forced to let go of him, and he escaped into the basement, where he had so many hidey-holes I'd never find him!

The movers arrived at 8:00 a.m. sharp.

"We'll just have to keep him locked in the basement and get him later," Pete said, in a tone of voice that pleaded *please don't argue.*

"But the movers won't be able to get the furniture in the basement," I pointed out. "Besides, we need to get both cats to the vet, and I wanted them brought to the new house together."

Pete and I got into the first of several—um, shall we say "intense"—discussions. I realized we were arguing right in front of the movers, who were waiting for us—at $160 an hour.

"Okay, go ahead and take Olaf to the vet, and I'll supervise the movers," I sputtered before announcing loudly to everyone, *"THIS DAY IS NOT GETTING OFF TO A VERY GOOD START!"*

For the next two hours the four men from the moving company tromped in and out of the house. At one point, my glass tabletop, which the movers had carelessly set against a wall with nothing to anchor it, came crashing down and shattered. I screamed loud enough to be heard down the block.

When everyone came in to see what was wrong, I told *them* to chill.

At the new house, the men had a hard time backing the moving van into the driveway, which had a sharp turn and—to make matters worse—was packed with snow and ice. The drivers were clearly irritated because they had to get out their shovels and clear some of the driveway so they could get the truck close enough to the house to unload it.

I was in a surly mood myself because I had warned them about the driveway when I called to set up the move, and had told them they needed to use one of their smaller trucks. I also reminded them that they were the ones who insisted on coming at 8:00 a.m. sharp, not 10:00 a.m.

as I had requested, so I could be more prepared, but who would listen to little old me anyway?

I berated myself. I should have postponed the move until some of the snow and ice melted. I should have taken my cats to the vet the night before.

When the movers finally got the last piece of furniture into the new house, I turned my attention back to the cats. Since it was only noon, maybe there was still time to get Champagne to the vet, and then I could bring both cats to their new home together as I had originally planned. Champagne started meowing indignantly as soon as I walked in the front door of the old house. I opened the door to the basement and let him upstairs. He came right up to me.

"Okay!" I thought. "Maybe now I can get him into the carrier."

No deal. He stayed close to me, but just out of reach.

I put a dish of his favorite canned food inside the carrier. While I waited for him to take the bait, I occupied myself by sorting items from the kitchen cabinets that still needed to be packed. After about fifteen minutes, to my delight, he did crawl into the carrier. I could hear him inside making little smacking noises as he nibbled the food. Quickly I reached down to close the door behind him. Alas! Once again, I had gotten in too much of a hurry. Once again, my growling, hissing, furious bundle of claws and teeth forced me to let him go.

I tried to think of alternatives. Maybe I could throw a sheet over him and capture him that way. I picked up a sheet and moved from room to room. When he followed me, I closed the doors to one room after another. Finally I had him trapped in the bedroom.

We circled each other.

Champagne growled and hissed.

I backed him into a corner and prepared to throw the sheet on top of him. He stopped growling and began to whimper, as if he were crying. He trembled as he cried.

The poor little thing is terrified, I realized.

Images ran through my mind of him cuddling in my lap just that morning, nuzzling my face and purring in my ear while I had my morning coffee. How long before he would do that again? Weeks? Months? I felt like I was betraying his earlier trust, but I couldn't even think of leaving him behind at the old house.

"Come on, baby," I cooed softly. "Please!"

He continued to cry.

Tears began rolling down my own cheeks. "I just want you to be with me at the new house," I pleaded.

I began to pray: "Please help me get him into the carrier. Please!"

I could picture the reaction from some of my friends if they knew what I was doing. I was calling on God to help me with a cat? Wasn't that kind of frivolous? And besides, why did I only call on God when I was in *trouble?*

Nevertheless, I continued to pray: "I love this little guy. Please show me what to do."

Then small miracles began to happen.

No, Champagne didn't hop into the carrier. But he did hop into a cardboard box half full of shoes.

V-E-R-Y S-L-O-W-L-Y, careful not to make any sudden moves this time, I pushed down the flaps and duct-taped the box shut, leaving just enough of a crack so he could get air but could not escape. We would simply have to skip the vet visit today, I decided, as I lugged the box—cat, shoes and all—to the car.

Champagne howled continually, all the way to the new house.

"You'll be all right," I reassured him, over and over.

I was beyond tired. The day had been so long and grueling! Maybe God was giving me a message about what happens when I try to force things, I thought. Our poor little kitties had been through a lot of turmoil in the past week with all the packing and moving going on. I would need to be extra nice to them. Cuddle them. Give them some extra treats and lots of attention.

When we got to our new home, Champagne at first didn't want to come out of the box that held him and the shoes. But he finally ventured out, and promptly hid behind a chair.

Pete went to the vet to pick up Olaf and when he came back, both cats began tentatively crawling around and sniffing their new surroundings. Pete put on some classical music. My frazzled nerves started to calm down.

I drove to the store to pick up some emergency supplies, including a fresh supply of kitty treats. In front of my windshield, as I drove along Outer Park Drive, was the most beautiful sunset! I calmed down even more and felt the tension drain from my neck and shoulders.

By nightfall, both cats had crawled into bed with us. Champagne seemed to have forgiven me already.

Yes, he's forgiven me, I thought, *but that whole standoff might not have happened if I hadn't been so impatient.*

Just that morning, while I was sipping my coffee and cuddling Champagne, I had written in my journal that I needed to slow down and not rush-rush-rush, and I needed to not let others pressure me into rushing either. I believe "Where's the fire?" was the theme.

"I can slow down now," I told myself, as I lay in bed snuggling with the cats and contemplating all the boxes I would need to start unpacking in the morning. There was plenty of time to get adjusted to our dream house. For both me and my kitties.

Debi Sue Edmund

THE DAY THE STORIES DIED

Last night I had the strangest dream.
The stories all had died.
The world became a better place.
No one cheated; no one lied.

All the countries of the world
Took great care to deflect
All conflict that could lead to war.
All were treated with respect.

And love was all around us
Each woman, child and man
Transmitted only kindness,
Did their best to understand.

And animals had naught to fear
For humans gave up meat.
The weather became calmer,
Storms rare and snow a treat.

And everyone lived happily
And felt most truly blessed,
Except for the poor writers,
They were unequal to the test.

For stories need a conflict
And no matter how they tried,
They couldn't write without it,
So that's why the stories died.

Linda McElroy

Legends of the Fall

Egyptian Columns
photograph
Linda McElroy

PATH

Around the lagoon, Path reaches to hold
vanquished June to her breast
one more time. Under walkers' rime,
children's skip, riders' tread,
her empty arms slip 'till at last she does
rest a darkly slumber,
    still her arms unfold
    still her arms remain
           outstretched.

Autumn etched, their parkas gray, damp,
a pair of fellow seekers slop confetti
flocked summer into space—
mandarin, umber, gold, chilly red.
Heavy they lumber in wool-socked
sneakers and elephantine grace,
    unaware of her pain
    unaware they tramp
          atop her embrace.

Jean Staff

LEGENDS OF THE FALL

Some say Eve's sexuality
Caused God's wrath and Adam's fall,
But speaking as a woman,
That was not the case at all.

What really caused the problem
Sealing mankind and their fate
Was not the snake's temptation,
But boredom with her mate.

Linda McElroy

LEGEND OF FALL

Adam and Eve
Fell upward
To the world
To life
Above the angels,

But ever after affected
By gravity
By birth pains
By paradise lost,

Searching for God
Hoping for heaven
Afraid of death

Celia Wesle

In the beginning
there was laughter
moon eyes and
natural face-lifts.
Contentment grew
with each chuckle that
radiated throughout every being.

Then Zeus bled Hera.
Shiva shook Shakti.
Adam kissed Eve.
Cain killed Abel.
And Tibet was taken.

Tears bore upon our beings
liquid Drano
for salvation.
A growing purge
in the stomach
of life, ruminating
through the entire self.

And it was said that the people
forgot–there were no sounds
spilling forth
from lungs or lips—
spreading joy—
no pleasant feelings—
goodwill toward men or women...

...the corporation was formed.

Anita Stienstra

TO MICHAEL

Michael Jackson represents what America is for many who aspire to be American—a dream of freedom to pursue and use what ever gifts have been bestowed on us. I was just making this observation last night when I attended my African son-in-law's church anniversary services at Faith International Ministries. They were celebrating five years in the formation of a church for Africans and anyone who chooses to worship with them. As each person ascended to the podium to give their history and testimony about becoming successful here in this country, I realized that through the eyes of an immigrant, America represents far more than perhaps those of use born here can imagine.

Michael Jackson, an African American, was able to show forth his gifts of song and dance, realize a dream of success, the American Dream. Thank you, Michael.

Jennifer C. Herring

Mysteries/Family Secrets

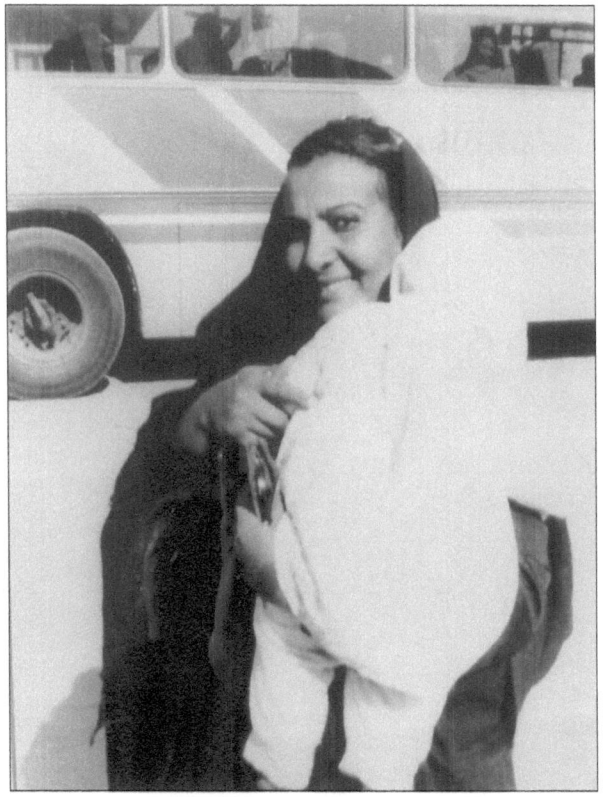

Mother on Street in Egypt
photograph
Celia Wesle

I'LL REMEMBER

just for today
I'll remember
what must be done
I'll remember

to write in my journal
take Annie out
wash dishes
I'll remember

to clean the bathroom
shower and wash my hair
make my bed
I'll remember

to get dressed
dry my hair
put on a little makeup
I'll remember

to do some stretches
run the vacuum
read
I'll remember

to eat lunch
take a nap
check e-mail
I'll remember

to do all those things
and if I don't
the sky won't fall
the earth won't shake

or if it does
I'll remember
my forgetting
didn't cause it

Pat Martin

LIVING WITH ALIENS

There was a time when I was sure I had given birth to aliens. In May of 1986, Hands Across America encouraged 5-1/2 million people to join hands in a 4,124-mile-long line from New York to Los Angeles. For fifteen minutes we were to hold hands, sing "Hands Across America" and form a human chain across America as part of the Bicentennial celebration. The event was designed to raise money for America's poor and homeless.

This was the kind of thing our family typically did. I wanted my children and myself to have this as a memory of interesting things we'd done as a family. But, being teenagers, they balked. They balked about going to the celebration, and it appeared since their dad and I divorced, they balked about everything. Lordy, Lordy, I was having a rough time being a parent, feeling love, and seeing these people as my children.

I wasn't as stressed by how things were with my sons, Marvin or Steven, but I was thoroughly disappointed with my relationship with Deana. I had such high hopes for our relationship. From the time she was born, I was sure we would be good friends and up until now, we had been. When she was younger, I sewed us matching dresses, allowed her to be around when I worked, and took her with me wherever I went. I was so proud to be her mother. She was sweet, cooperative, and beautiful.

As things changed, our relationship was filled with potholes and destructive exchanges. My heart was heavy and my eyes leaked bitter tears. I tried to keep my mouth shut. I didn't want to say the things that were in my head that I couldn't take back.

For the celebration, Deana didn't want to be seen with me. She had the admiration of her peers, and her friends; she didn't need a mother. And by golly, she went all out.

The first big change was outward. She became obsessed with doing things to her body and seeing how it looked to others. Fashion, makeup, hairstyles were important, and they changed her identity. She cut fenders in her hair around her ears making them look like Ford tractor wheels. She wore all black clothes.

The second change was in her relationships. They were unstable and unpredictable. We began to fight about everything and often. She distanced herself from me and began identifying with groups of kids I called losers. Her motor-mouthed talk was about her new friends, latest gossip, how fine some guy's body was and how easy he would be to get. It was hard to listen to. When I tried to make appropriate suggestions, she let me know she had friends, she didn't need my old-fashioned advice.

The third change was her reputation. Pretty soon, rumors

began to fly about her drinking, using drugs, and having sex freely and indiscriminately. It was rumored that she would sleep with any warm body if she had enough to drink. She was accused of consuming alcohol in large quantities and shamelessly flirting with guys, usually ones who already had a girlfriend.

I had struggled to maintain a peaceful stance but with this information, I lost it. Early one morning during yet another entangled battle with her, I hurled the closest thing at hand; a steaming pot full of coffee, aiming for her head. I regretted that I missed her and hit the wall. About that time, I knew I had gone too far and took us both to see a therapist.

Even though I had provided psychotherapy to others for many years, I learned a few things in the therapist's office. There's a fine line between love and hate, both can be destructive—the passion that propels you in one direction can easily propel you in the other—and as a newly divorced woman, Deana and I were in the same confusing place on the road, but travelling in different directions. She was heading excitedly into the freedom of early adulthood, I was trying to figure out how to pick up the pieces and go on with my life. While she was looking forward to life with increasing zest, I was trying to figure out how to use their dwindling energies. I was confused and she challenged my confusion. She opened me up to face my fears that I had effectively hidden within myself so deep I no longer had to face them or work on them.

I realized that my adult relationships weren't stable either. After breaking up with the kids' father and being on the dating scene, I was questioning my ability to maintain relationships. Though middle age, I was starting over. My life was half over. If I hadn't achieved my dream, I'd better get busy. As the kids broke away from me, I had to move forward on my own journey.

Finally, because I had teenage children in the house, I felt restrained in developing my newfound sexuality. I had to be responsible, consistent and set a good model. This was a tall order but, I held myself to very high, though confusing standards. It was clear I had to redirect my thinking. I know I'd given my children roots, now I'd have to give them wings. That was hard but I vowed to try. I was determined though, to make the Hands Across America celebration, with my children by my side. But Hands Across America was having growing pains that resembled ours. According to news reports, because of the massive scale of the project, there were breaks in the line. Organizers were working hard with each other to connect the 200 separate lines into the massive coast-to-coast line. With determination and cooperation, 5-1/2 million people joined hands in a 4,124-mile-long line from New York to Los Angeles. It is not known exactly how much money was raised by Hands Across America, but the event brought together people of all races, creeds, and religions for a 15-minute period of harmony.

The project was symbolic. It reminded me that there is no standing still on the journey on life. You have to move on or you lose. But if you work hard with direction and determination and in cooperation with others, you'll get the job done.

By Thanksgiving, the battles had subsided. Marvin had gone to the military. Steven was in college and enjoying courses in photography. Deana hit the road traveling from Illinois to California fueled only by her thumb and I dare imagine, what other body parts. Me, I was so heartbroken and full of sorrow that even the annual Thanksgiving gathering with the family was no solace. And there was nothing I could do but pray.

Rachell N. Anderson

THREE KINDS OF SECRETS

Your secret curls up under the couch by the fireplace
like a cat content after eating and no care in the world.
It sneaks under your covers late at night
startles you as you half wake—feel fur—
and remember you live alone. You have no cat.

Your secret hides in the shed outside by the woodpile.
You placed it there years ago for safe keeping—
for protection—those secrets minimize harm
to yourself and others. They are forgotten
for a reason, stored away for good.

Your secret snores on the braided rug
grandma crafted by the hearth like a dog
dreaming of chasing a cat. It jumps up
by you in bed at night and the slight touch,
the depression in the covers, is as familiar

and reassuring as a parent's love. Your secret
lives in your life, in your house. It roams there
because you own it. You have nothing to hide.
Some secrets are fascinating creatures
that are merely undiscovered facts.

Anita Stienstra

Uncle was a gruff, loud spoken, sometimes crude man who aired his opinions about Negras, Catholics, Jews, homosexuals, Asians, Mexicans, and women to anyone in shouting distance. "None of them are worth a G.D___!" was one of his milder rants. "You don't mean that," Aunt would say taking son and daughter by the hands out to play on the bag swing hanging from the big oak. Pretty much an absentee father, he spent most of his time at the bowling alley he owned or cleaning his passion—a collection of carnival items. Aunt painted beautiful landscapes at the kitchen table when he doled out money for supplies and a was a stay-at-home mom raising two well-behaved children. He had piercing black eyes with no sign of softness and cruel lips that never smiled. She was soft spoken, and frequently smiled. Their only car was a 1949 Plymouth. that she was not allowed to drive. They lived in sleepy small-town Missouri in a modest well-cared-for duplex house, renting out the "other side" to a long-term renter to supplement their income.

Aunt purchased marked-down groceries, clipped coupons, saved green stamps, grew a vegetable garden. She cut the family's hair and shopped for clothes at a thrift shop, never owning a new dress. Uncle expressed pride that they never shopped retail nor took vacations. "Don't believe in insurance, banks, or the G.D. commie government in power." For years the family and neighbors debated whether they had no money at all or had a fortune hidden somewhere in the house. We cousins speculated as to where — "in the basement with the carnival memorabilia," whispered Rick. "Under Uncle's fat mattress in his bedroom," "I know where it is," I boasted, "there must be a safe behind the brick wall in the kitchen."

As years passed the rumors grew until half the town believed the couple had millions of dollars in gold coins buried in the backyard. People whispered about it in their kitchens, at the soda shop, grocery store, the town square.

Yet for them frugal life went on. Aunt won a blue ribbon for her meatless meatloaf at the county fair. She continued painting landscapes and must have had thirty or forty stored in the attic. "Don't think they're good enough to sell, but I would like to frame them," she lamented. "Hell, I'm not spending any more of my money on that garbage!" he barked.

At Uncle's insistence the children were on their own after high-school graduation. "Don't need to be under my roof. Not gonna support your lazy asses anymore. Get your own place." After that Aunt began taking the train to St. Louis to visit her children and then grandchildren. She spoke less and less to Uncle and painted more and more. Often in their housedresses and saddle shoes, Aunt and Renter, would sit on the front porch swing drinking iced tea, venting and discussing a couple of rumors.

Uncle took to traveling with carnivals and might be gone weeks at a time once he retired. Aunt and Renter walked to the A & P, the Goodwill, and the local crossroads restaurant where she began displaying and selling her paintings. Summer evenings they sat on the porch swing drinking Long Island ice-tea, excitedly dreaming, reading about empowerment, feminism, equal rights, discussing ideas.

After a time, the rumors had pretty much abated. At the age of 65, Uncle had a stroke and died instantly. Aunt bought a new black Buick and a black pants-suit from Saks Fifth Avenue for the funeral. Three weeks later Aunt bought a new house. She had a few specifications: a large room with lots of windows and a skylight for her studio, two guest rooms for kids and grands and anyone she hoped would visit, a spacious master suite for herself and the renter.

Later through the realty company we learned she had paid for the house $550,000...in cash.

Jean Staff

Always Wonder

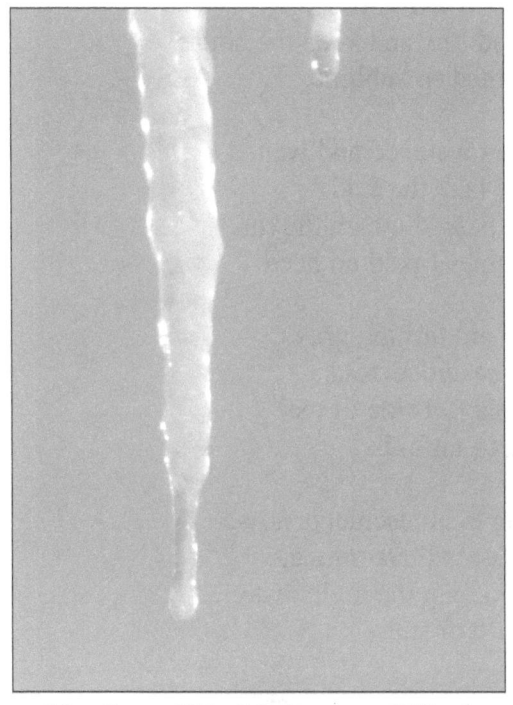

The Incredible Lightness of Water
photograph
Anita Stienstra

ALWAYS WONDER

When I was born in autumn,
My goal was to be grown.
I worked and had no time for play,
My seeds of fun unsown.

I could not wait to be adult
And prove myself in time.
To cook and sew and keep the house
To me seemed so sublime.

My brothers watched and waited
And let me take the lead.
My sisters passed me on the run.
To their games I paid no heed.

Now that I am turning gray,
Or should be so I'm told,
I find the playful side of me
Beginning to unfold.

I'm turning to amusements now.
My playmates all are young.
We talk and plan the night away
Until the rise of sun.

My life seems to run backward.
Each day new wonders bring
And now when winter lurks nearby,
I laugh and think of spring.

Linda McElroy

RIGHT OUTSIDE MY WINDOW

Snowflakes accumulate
right outside my window,
the window of my soul.

I open up to receive
the thoughts of pleasure
contrasting with the cold,
stark whiteness of my environment.
Brown, hard trees stand firm
right outside my window,
the window of my soul,

waiting on me to choose which
one will be selected to provide
the warmth of fire to calm
my frazzled senses, to singe my soul,

I am here, ready to do this,
Comfort me, O God.

Jennifer C. Herring

FLIRT OF FLICKERING FIREFLIES

on the Sangamon
hundreds
of male
fireflies
wink in unison
through navy
august night

across the
riverbank
hundreds
of female
fireflies
return
the splendid
unison winks

the flirt of
flickering
fireflies
pulsing against a
blanket of dark
excites
voyeurs
like me

Jean Staff

ALWAYS WONDER

I am filled with wonder
Reverence and awe
For great conditions of nature:
The large lake,
The smooth round stones it has made
And laid
Along its edge,
A bright blue sky spotted
Through clumps of yellow leaves,
The summer greens underfoot and overhead,
Lilac fragrance that envelops me,
Michigan's high sand dunes,
Holland's mighty fields of tulips,
Being part of a large crowd of excited people,
Inspiring teachers at college
My wonder continues.

Celia Wesle

THE PEACE HOOK UP

It starts within, that small still yearning to make things right and welcome for yourself, as well as those around you. I began this journey for peace by learning to recognize rather quickly those who are on this quest as well. I look for the peacemakers everywhere I go.

The peacemaker's peace is there in a quiet unhurried smile, a knowing look of self-content, self-assurance. The peacemaker's speech is solid, careful, yet free-flowing. There is a residue of long suffering words, well-said, non-offensive, yet true. The peacemaker's speech is not a long, boring one, not one riddled with brash selfish, it's-all-about-me words. The peacemaker's speech is one of heal-ing, counselor lexis, very therapeutic, not clamorous.

When I locate a peacemaker, I make a connection as quickly as possible. That way, I am connecting my power to theirs, acknowledging the goodness of woman (and man). This is the goodness of woman (and man), that uncanny ability to make big peace piles by hook-ups, one person af-ter the other, plugging into each other's power of love. Hook-ups start by simple acts of kindness, not big Macy, Neiman-Marcus purchases, not you scratch my back, I'll scratch yours—just simple acts of kindness. It is about al-lowing a car to suddenly cross over in my lane, in front of me with no ready explanation as to why that driver did that. What was he (or she) thinking?

Jennifer C. Herring

Springtime

Morning Glories
painting
Kimberly Magowan

PULLED BY PASSION INTO SPRING

We overfed the hunger.
It turned into passion
then pulled us onward
to where we should have stood all along.

Timid muscles moved to speak
and days called to months, then years
paradise revisited, remade into
how your name and mouth fit between my lips.

You instill in me, the first sight of redbuds
full upon a blank winter cold.
Your color warms in me moments
so long lost, and yet new, unpacked after frost.

I may never own a redbud or kiss you again
but in all seasons your memory touches me
our skin entwines with the same sun and stars
and our love like a tree, blooms away any scars.

Anita Stienstra

What is more compelling than the
softness of a perennial as it
reappears after having been
laying down, out of the way,
in the recesses of the dark earth
for so long?

Day by day it begins to flower
pushing forth, past the rain
and the thunder, past the
rushing mighty winds, up toward
the sun it looks and lives
out its love, being a friend
to whomever smells it, picks it.

At long last the love is shared,
the friendship blossoms as
the winter darkness goes away
and this spring's forget-me-nots
show up.

Jennifer C. Herring

HEALER

Laying hands

on rows pinch eyed

standing froze or caravan,

even those muse mummified,

in whispered hues she began

to heal the song-still countryside.

As she passed, long last beheld,

a hum arose from beasties stirred.

A hum that lauding thankful welled.

Plaiting strum, note, drum and word,

hum swelled and swelled and swelled

till a chorus great could be heard,

  "Hallelujah,   Spring has come!"

Jean Staff

My child phones from Alabama. She hears
the warning siren. *I gotta go now, right now.* She hangs up.
I know the drill. She'll grab
her psychedelic red roller-blade helmet.
Crawl under the downstairs vanity. Hugging
her knees she'll hear the proverbial freight train above her
prayer,
Don't let it come closer.

At last she calls back. Just before her block,
she says, it touched down, ripped off
balconies, shattered windows. Jumped
to the Black Warrior River. Lifted a speed-
boat. Hurled it onto the highway overpass.
Then it sucked all the windows out
of the corner station where she stops
every morning to buy a paper.

She says twenty miles north another twister
obliterated Carbon Hill's elementary school.
Three people died. Says she's worn out.
Gonna curl up on the couch, beneath
her favorite soft-nap blanket. Close
her eyes. Says another storm's already
on its way. Soon it'll reach Tuscaloosa.
I say, *Call back.*

Click. Dial tone. Silence.
The rest of the night tulips
of Holland fill the screen
of the weather channel.
I guess there's nothing
important to report.
Near dawn I fall asleep,
still holding the phone.

Pat Martin

FOND FAREWELL

There
Have been wary times
But mostly joys in loving you.
Even if I could, it would be greedy
To implore for more,
As I say, "Goodbye."

I
Wonder why or how
I could have prolonged the song.
That delightful way to be
Came not from your love of me.
I see it was my heart
Made true, expanding to you.

Do
Remember me;
I'll think about having been filled
From hair to heel
With pleasure in your presence,
With admiration of your goodness,
With thanksgiving for your friendship.

Celia Wesle

True Sisters

Women Writers Association

WRITING WITH THE WOMEN

It must have looked weird to my sister Julia when she and her Grandson, Shawn, approached us on the back porch of my new house knee to knee. The five of us were sitting, facing the wind, looking at the sunset, and reading stuff that had been on our minds for at least a month. We were so involved with each other, we hardly noticed Julia and Shawn approach.

Too, it must have looked weird to strangers when we women met in Washington Park or sat on Celia's patio writing stories as the wind whipped our papers around as it did with hurricanes Katrina and Rita. Some of us actually wrote about those hurricanes because most of us had left a part of our heart in New Orleans and knew we would not live long enough to get those parts back.

We may appear to be weird but for the past 26 years, this small group of women has been writing, reading and putting on shows for the world to see. Meeting in parks, each other's homes, in museums, we have dedicated ourselves to words because we believe words have the power to create conditions for our lives. As I look back on the conditions of my life, I have to acknowledge the gifts I received from writing with the women.

When I joined the group, I had a lot to say but I didn't have a voice. Sure I had written things. I had kept a journal for years. I started with and loitered in poetry for awhile. That was fun but soon, I moved on. I wrote essays, then articles, a dissertation, and books. Presently, I believe my talent is in writing stories. But that could evolve yet again.

Listening to my group members read their writing helped me to find my voice. They listened to me too. This wasn't always easy. But it was those ears that allowed me to see an idea, a phrase, a character, or a sentence in a different way—making it possible to love it or change it. They supported me in my writing and in my life. I learned to make dreams for my life by using their eyes and ears. No, they didn't know I was doing that, but I was. It seemed that whenever I talked about an idea or a project with the women, it became doable, and I'd go out and do it.

At first, becoming a part of the group was hard for me. Fearing judgment and protective of my fragile verse, I tread with soft-soled feet. At times, I wanted to read the works of great people rather than my own. I'd have writers block during our free writing exercises. I'd gripe, complain, and sometimes came late to meetings. Through it all, not one woman complained about me (at least not to me).

Becoming a woman writer was much like coalescing into womanhood. I grew up in a family of women and have worked for pay all my adult life, raised a family, and was actively involved in the women's movement during the 60s, 70s, and 80s. I was a part of the marches on Springfield and Washington and wore the tee shirts with the $0.59 logo. Yet, claiming my womanhood was a different process.

Today, I find it hard to look in the unaware or unappreciative faces of young women who think they have always been able to go to school for degrees in law, medicine, and psychology when and where they please, and get the pay they now receive. Many slough it off as olden times and maybe those times are forever in the past. I feel sad when I hear women unable to see through the shallow veil and spew their prejudices against other women saying they never want a woman boss because she is bitchy or emotional. As I have grown to recognize and reclaim the special talents of my mother, sisters, aunts, and all other women in my life, I can firmly ask them if they'd want to be a boss someday.

At some point I buckled down in group and began writing for understanding in a similar way I claimed my woman-ness. As I gained self understanding, I discovered truths about myself and my abilities. I have been able to resolve conflicts that had festered for more than half century. I don't believe these resolutions could have happened had I not been writing. My heart opened wider. I began to feel more love for people and received more love from them. I also discovered that I loved to write primarily because of what it can do.

About the Women Writer's group, many have come and gone. Some have died. Others have lost interest but new ones come and we continue.

Me, I write every day. It has become a habit and a part of who I am. Because I write, I am a much nicer person. I look forward to every meeting. If not there in person, I'm there in spirit.

If someone thinks we look weird, I think, so be it.

Rachell N. Anderson

CHICKEN

The dialysis nutritionist's chart
Itemizes my lacks and toxins,
I walk among you, ladies of the hen house,
See your young, limber drumsticks,
Can you see my grateful gaze?

I don't want your fright feelings
To send struggle hormones
Into your muscles or eggs
Nixing the healthy effects of
Open range and organic grains.

Can you look at me with quiet eyes?
As I bless you with God's grace
And thank you for your life
That gifts my frail body
With potent protein.

Celia Wesle

Reality and Illusions

Stars in My Coffee, Brain Games, Aliens, Light and God
photograph
Anita Stienstra

WALKING INTO HER SHADOW

When the mower stopped and she
missed the noise, she knew for sure
she had gone mad.

Yesterday she walked into her shadow.
She had chased it as a kid
but never entered its darkness.

It waited on the wall, stayed in
one position, did not run
did not evade her when she approached.

It seemed to beckon her now as if it was time.
One can always enter light
it stands as open as a mother's arms.

The dark cowers in corners
that disappear when you move toward it.
But not now, the shadow sits still.

When the mower stopped, when the noise ceased
men with heavy lips moved back and forth around the lawn.
They worked hard to scrap her from the grass.

Anita Stienstra

MADNESS AT PERDIDO BEACH

It was as if the tv was drunk,
flashing on its own from channel
to channel, chasing its volume
back and forth across the screen.
After your good whack it settled
on one station long enough for us
to watch the NCAA basketball
semifinal, Kansas vs Maryland.

Then the sleep timer—the one we couldn't find any
way to program—
kicked on. You were snoring
and I couldn't stop the countdown.
With :08 to go, the tv shut off,
Maryland in the lead by 5 and Kansas,
I think, having called a time out
they didn't have coming.

I was hoping the tv would work right
this morning so I could find out who
won the game, but it's still cycling,
frantic as that banner streaming
behind a cockamamie skywriter:
Bubba's Seafood We got crab legs!

Pat Martin

REALITY/ILLUSION

Last winter a snowflake
Landed on my hand.
While I watched
It disappeared.
Had it been real?
Of course.
It just changed forms.

Is love real?
Does it show up on
Pictures of brain cells?
Most of us have had
The sad experience
Of deciding it had been an illusion.
Hence diverse.

Isobel Allende
Of Chili, South America
Is described by her reviewers
As writing magic realism.
She answers
"Magic." No!
There are several
Kinds of realism;
They all operate
At the same time.

We know a solid table
Is made of moving atoms:
Energy with a nucleus.
Everything thought of as real
Is actually energy.
Are souls energy?
Is God energy?
Is the world and
Our experiences illusions?
Many questions.

Celia Wesle

THE NIGHT THE MAGIC DIED

Barefooted, I whirled in soggy
July-green grass, Minnie-Mouse
nightie flowing near translucent
beneath moon shadow—
ballerina, angel, ghostly hunter.

Golden lid with air hole speckles
clutched in one chubby hand,
glass jar in the other, I clapped
them together over and over again,
catching lightning bugs one at a
time, sometimes two until morphed
a *m*agic jar.
Twinkling glittering flickering.

Setting it on the dresser, I smiled
into bed. Mother tucked me in
and shut off the lamp to dreaded
darkness. I turned my head
and, heavy lidded, gazed at
the *m*agic jar—

twinkling glittering flickering.
twinkling glittering flickering.

Dream laden excitement and slats
of sun through the blinds snapped
eyes wide open. Little toes,
dirty green wiggled "good morning"
from under the spread.
I turned my head, on the dresser—
a canning jar full of dead bugs….

The night the magic died.

Jean Staff

87

THE DINNER DANCE

Rod Stewart played in the background as she got ready. His deep growling voice made her sway her ample hips and toss back her layered hair in what she was sure was a Donna Summer-like move. She squeezed the bottle of lotion into her hands and ran the liquid over her skin, seeing a bronze glow that made her smile.

"Tonight's the night," she crooned along with Rod as she slipped into the summer dress that felt like silk. Fluffing her hair and checking her makeup one last time she headed for the kitchen. The lasagna was almost done. The salad was finished, rolls were browned, and the bottle of wine was chilling.

He walked into the kitchen and her heart quickened as he looked her over from head to toe and whispered, "Oh my."

The hands she knew so well, had known in fact for more than three decades, held hers and pulled her close. He danced her out of the kitchen into the dining room and crooned, "Just let your inhibitions run wild," along with Rod.

They swayed around the table tripping just a bit over the dog that refused to move and their granddaughter's playpen that was wedged into the corner. Pictures of their children, spouses, and their granddaughter and grandson filled the buffet as they whirled past. Rod clicked off, and Carole King's voice filled the room with the rendition of "Tapestry."

"My life has been a tapestry of rich and royal hue," she sang into his ear. She ran her fingers through the hair that had been golden wheat when they met. He tilted his head sure she could see the desire in his eyes as she continued the song as her hands caressed the back of his neck.

"If you ever thought of going into singing, don't," he whispered back over their long standing joke that her voice didn't sound quite the same outside of her head as it did inside. She continued to sing at the top of her voice the rest of the words to the song that she knew so well and loved.

She looked at a picture of the two of them taken on a trip. They stood young, thin and golden with the sun glowing behind their heads. "We haven't changed a bit," she sighed, and he just smiled.

In his eyes, she was as beautiful as the day they married. "There is just a bit more of us to love," he added pulling her to him.

They stepped over the log of a dog one more time and he settled a deep kiss on her then twirled her into the kitchen where the smell of lasagna overcame his dance desire. He ran his hands up and down her back and settled them momentarily on her backside. After a soft pat and his deep inhalation of breath and admiring look at the golden bubbling cheese she took the hint and handed him the wine to pour them a glass for dinner. As they dined, he took a bite of lasagna and bread slathered with butter. Waving his fork he mouthed, "I love you."

This wasn't quite the moment she hoped to hear those words. She pictured the turned-down bed, the candles burning on the nightstand, and the romantic card on his pillow that she had sealed an hour before. He waved the breadstick at her and leered. She smiled, seeing the humor in the moment, for in truth, the reality was much better than the illusion. She said, "I love you too," as they finished the wine and dished up the dessert.

Cindy Ladage

Women Writers Association
Springfield Motor Boat Club, 2010

THE AUTHORS

Dr. Rachell N. Anderson is professor emeritus, author, and a licensed clinical psychologist who ran a private clinical practice in Springfield, Illinois from 1974 until she retired in July 2008. For twenty years, Dr. Anderson taught clinical courses to graduate students and served as chair of the Department of Human Services at the University of Illinois at Springfield. She has lectured widely, served as vice president and chair of the publications committee for the North American Society of Adlerian Psychology. Dr. Anderson has received many awards for learning, teaching, healing, and serving in her field including, but not limited to: The Committee For Children; Who's Who Among America's Teachers; Who's Who America's Professionals; Executives and Professional 2009 Woman of the Year; and the University's Pearson Faculty Award ,voted on by her peers. The honor carried a substantial monetary award of which Dr. Anderson donated a portion via 20 copies of her book *Responsible Children in Today's World* to 50 daycare centers in her home state of Mississippi following Hurricane Katrina. She presently teaches a Writers Workshop at the Tunica Museum in Mississippi. Dr. Anderson has authored seven books including her most recent books: *Before Our Eyes* and *The Legacy Continues: Writing Healing Stories.* Her newest book, *Run Turkeys, Run* is due out by Thanksgiving.

Debi Sue Edmund is clinical program coordinator for a prison re-entry program in Springfield. Prior to her career as a counselor, she was a newspaper and magazine writer and editor. Her articles and short stories have appeared in regional and national publications, and she has won awards from The Associated Press, the Mississippi Valley Writer's Conference, and the Springfield Area Arts Council. She lives in Springfield with her husband Pete Ellertsen and her calico cat Angela.

Jennifer C. Herring, PhD Jennifer C. Herring is assistant professor in Teacher Education at the University of Illinois at Springfield. She also teaches online education courses at Duplichain University and the University of North Texas. Her interests are in the areas of multicultural education, technology, and health education. She has presented at numerous conferences and workshops. She is currently the chapter president of the Illinois-National Association for Multicultural Education. Her other interests include international travel to Africa, Canada, Mexico, China, and England. She loves freelance writing of poetry, prose, and has written a memoir, using her own voice, titled *Preacher's Daughter, Preacher's Kids, Church Kids: the phenomenon of growing up crazy in the Apostolic Pentecostal Church,* self-published and available at lulu.com.

Cindy Ladage is a freelance writer who works part-time for the state of Illinois. Ladage's latest novel is *Fairy Tales Are Fragile,* and the 2009 winner of the Timeless Romance Contest from Oak Tree Press. Ladage is also the author of *Where Did Laurita Go?* and *Love Forward.* Ladage also composed three short story collections, *Porch Swing Tales I, II,* and *III.* Along with Nokomis resident Jane Aumann, Cindy has also written two children's farm storybooks *Tucker's Surprise* and *The Christmas Tractor.* They have two more children's books in the works.

Linda McElroy A founding member of Women Writers Association, Linda has been a teacher, editor, speechwriter, and consultant. Her stories have won awards in the citywide competition On My Own Time and have been published in the *Alchemist Review, All the Women Were Heroes,* and *Mosaics.* Realizing that she was a better talker than writer, Linda turned to screenwriting and wrote, directed, and acted in *The Perfect Mark* which played at film festivals across the country. She is currently the director of the Route 66 International Film Festival in Springfield and works on local film productions.

Kimberly K. (Steil) Magowan Born in San Jose, CA, Kimberly is a portrait artist living in Springfield, Illinois with her three sons. She earned an Associate of Arts degree from Springfield College in Illinois and completed her Bachelor degree at the University of Illinois at Springfield. She is an art teacher at both St. Agnes and St. Patrick's Grade schools and teaches fine art classes to children and adults for other city organizations. In the past, Kimberly has served as a board of directors member for the Springfield Area Arts Council, as Event Coordinator for Michaels, and as an art teacher at ARC at Boaden Adult Center where she had the rewarding job of teaching art to severely, mentally-handicapped adults, and those with Alzheimer's and Parkinson's disease. Kimberly also exhibits each year at The Festival of Trees, several auctions, and the SHG Mostaccioli Dinner, and has given many presentations and speeches on fine art for organizations that include The Rembrandt Society and the AARP. Her business, Oil Portraits by Kimberly, thrives as her work has been commissioned by many clients and businesses throughout the city including Christ the King Church, Gold's Gym, and Bergners, who received 32 paintings in 2006.

Pat Martin is a central Illinois writer who divides her time between Taylorville and Springfield, Illinois. Some of her stories and poems appear in the anthologies *At the Edges of Our Comfort* and *All the Women Were Heroes.* Other poems have appeared in *Eureka Literary Magazine* and *Illinois_Times.* She has recently published a book, *Needles of Light,* a collection of poems written over a twenty-year period beginning in the mid 80s. In addition, she was featured a number of times on public access television's weekly show, Works in Progress, produced by Peg Knoepfle, and has participated in numerous local public readings. She has a Bachelor degree from Eastern Illinois University, has taken a number of graduate level classes at the University of Illinois at Springfield, and has attended many writing workshops around the country.

Kathleen O'Hara Podzimek is the owner/operator of Wordsmith, a writing business. Kathleen has authored many grant applications and interactive murder mysteries and has also been published in literary works, including *Word Sorcery*, her book of poetry, as well as in *Brew's Muse, Caprice, Downstate Story*, and more. Kathleen has held many professional positions, including part-time Executive Director of Tourism for Menard County; part-time Teacher/Supervisor for the University of Illinois at Springfield; Program Administrator for Illinois State Board of Education; Assistant Principal for the Chicago Board of Education, and more. Kathleen lives in Petersburg with husband, Raymond, and their dog, Kee Kee.

Jean Staff began writing in the first grade when she wrote, illustrated, and colored a Christmas poem. She wrote a column for the *San Pan* in the sixties and has been published in the *Illinois Times, Prism, Vintage Visions,* and *Post Mortem Musings.* Serving on the board of directors for Poets and Writers Literary Forum and now Springfield Poets and Writers treasurer, she participated in Poetry Parnassus and Fiction Faction for over three years. Widowed by a jazz musician and retired as an advocate for abused women and their children at a local domestic violence shelter, she was also on the planning committee and participated in the *Take Back the Night* marches in 1991 and 1992. Upon meeting Gloria Steinem, she spent ten minutes of fame blinking, as flash bulbs popped, and stuttering "H-H-Hello" to her gracious hero. She is most proud of her four grandchildren, three grown children, a daughter of her heart. Jean lives in Springfield, Illinois with a giant black bipolar cat named Sparkles Muldoon, aka Sparky, who sometimes hisses, sometimes cuddles and an ancient computer named Alien who sometimes hisses, sometimes deletes. She still misses her home on the pond but relocated when the 46 beloved resident ducks were replaced by almost as many baggy-panted gang members.

Anita Stienstra is editor/publisher of Adonis Designs Press; editor of an annual teen poetry anthology, *The Maze*; president of Springfield Poets and Writers; and calendar editor at *Illinois Times*. Besides conducting poetry workshops, she has read extensively at regional venues such as: schools, libraries, festivals, bookstores, and on TV and radio. She taught writing and literature at two colleges and led literacy programs for teachers, caregivers, and students. Educated at DePauw University and the University of Illinois at Springfield, she holds a MA and BA in English with a concentration in poetry and poetics. Her poetry and photographs have been published in reviews, newspapers, five chapbooks, and most recently in *Focus Midwest, Today's Caregiver Magazine,* and the book, *Voices of Multiple Sclerosis*. Awards include Springfield Arts Council Artist Advancement Award, P&WLF President's Award, and Springfield Chamber of Commerce Athena Nominee Award.

Celia Wesle is an artist and writer, retired from the Illinois State Board of Education where she worked for sixteen years. At the University of Wisconsin-Milwaukee, she was the literary journal's poetry editor. In Beloit, Wisconsin, she taught for two years and was a librarian and modern dance teacher at Central College. She received a Master of Arts degree in counseling and guidance upon moving with her family to Normal, Illinois. After being accepted into the Doctoral program at Illinois State University in art education and completing several courses, she accepted the position of Educational Consultant with the ISBE. In 2008, the University of Illinois at Springfield College of Liberal Arts and Sciences, in conjunction with the University of Illinois Alumni Association, recognized Celia for the John Knoepfle Creative Writing Award—Poetry 2008. Her poetry has appeared in *Cheshire*, *Friend of Silence*, *All the Women Were Heroes*, *Stop the Violence*, the TV program *Works in Progress,* and in her recently published book of original art and poetry titled, *Light: Paintings and Poems*, that is a Brainchild Award Series book.

RiverBank **Lodge**
522 S. 6th St.
Petersburg, IL 62675

Richard D. Moss
Phone: (217) 632-0202
       (866) 459-3040
Cell: (217) 632-3130
www.riverbanklodge.com

Thank You to Our Sponsors

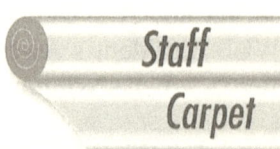

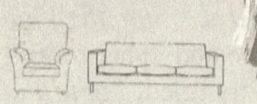

Thank You to Our Sponsors

 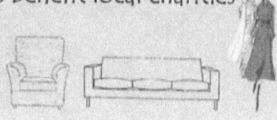
Thank You to Our Sponsors

TEXT INDEX BY AUTHOR

www.ingramcontent.com/pod-product-compliance
Lightning Source LLC
Chambersburg PA
CBHW020629130626
46552CB00003B/1148